Cloud, Stone, Sun, Vine

Cloud, Stone, Sun, Vine

Poems, Selected and New
By MAY SARTON

NEW YORK
W · W · NORTON & COMPANY · INC ·

FOR

Basil de Selincourt

Author's Note

These poems of twenty years have been arranged by theme not chronology into eight groups, and selected from four books: *Inner Landscape*, Houghton Mifflin, 1938; *The Lion and The Rose*, Rinehart and Co., 1948; *The Land of Silence*, Rinehart and Co., 1953, and *In Time Like Air*, Rinehart and Co., 1958.

The ninth section contains twenty-seven new poems. The sonnet sequence, "A Divorce of Lovers" appeared in the Centenary issue of *The Cornhill*, London; "Moving In" in *The Massachusetts Review;* "Mud Season" in *The Bryn Mawr Alumnae Bulletin;* "Spring Planting" in *Poetry: London-New York;* "Reflections by a Fire" in *The Virginia Quarterly Review*, "A Flower-Arranging Summer" in *The Lyric*, and "Der Abschied" in *The Kenyon Review*.

Contents

"Angels, often invoked, become a fact.
And they have names: Cloud, Stone, Sun, Vine". . . .

Prayer Before Work

Great one, austere,
By whose intent the distant star
Holds its course clear,
Now make this spirit soar—
Give it that ease.

Out of the absolute,
Abstracted grief, comfortless, mute,
Sound the clear note,
Pure, piercing as the flute:
Give it precision.

Austere, great one,
By whose grace the inalterable song
May still be wrested from
The corrupt lung:
Give it strict form.

American Places

A New Mexican Sequence

MEDITATION IN SUNLIGHT

1

In space in time I sit
Thousands of feet above
The sea and meditate
On solitude on love

Near all is brown and poor
Houses are made of earth
Sun opens every door
The city is a hearth

Far all is blue and strange
The sky looks down on snow
And meets the mountain range
Where time is light not shadow

Time in the heart held still
Space as the household god
And joy instead of will
Knows love as solitude

Knows solitude as love
Knows time as light not shadow
Thousands of feet above
The sea where I am now.

This landscape does not speak,
Exists, is simply there,
Take it or leave it; the weak
Suffer from fierce air.

For these high desolate
Lands where earth is skeleton
Make no demands; they state.
Who can resist the stone?

Implacable tranquillity
That searches out the naked heart,
Touches the quick of anxiety,
And breaks the world apart.

The angel in the flaming air
Is everywhere and no escape,
Asking of life that it be pure
And given as the austere landscape.

And most accompanied when alone;
Most sensitive when mastered sense;
Alive most when the will is gone,
Absence become the greatest Presence.

Without the violence, the major shift,
The shudder of the earth's foundations torn,
Without the great upheaval that could lift
That fiery core, it would not have been born,
And yet when chaos cooled, this land was here,
Absolute and austere—
Then, not before,
It snowed.
Later, by centuries and centuries
The saving water flowed,
The grass arrived, dark little trees.
After a terrible and rending war,
This land took on its fearful peace,
After, and not before.

1

Time beats like a heart; we do not hear it
But we are nourished as by sleep after pain.
Death is so close to life that we can bear it.
The smallest veins drink time and breathe again.

2

Now I am here in the land of silence,
Of the near dove and the distant hills,
I know that the surface is the essence,
No stripping down what is already bare,
No probing what is absolutely here.
This is the land of bones and violent dreaming
Where Heaven is woven in and out of Hell
And each not essence but actual and near.

Even more than love we search for faith
Who in this high air must gasp for breath.

Was it a long journey for you to begin
To grow peaceful green things,
To harvest well, to watch the sun
Go down, to find the ancient springs?
What human pain, what wild desire
Did you burn in the fire,
Long ago, Tilano?

What is the first step, Tilano,
Toward the wisdom of your feet,
Treading the dust or the snow
So quiet, so tender, so fleet?
I have come from far
To the warm sun and the shelter,
A long journey to reach here,
And now it is clear
That I do not know
The first step.

What is the first act, Tilano,
Toward the wisdom of your hands?
They plant the corn;
They bring in the lamp in the evening,
Wood for the fire, and each thing done
With rigorous love, with devotion.
It was a long journey to you and the sun,
And now it seems I clasp in your hand
A land of work and silence, a whole land.

What is the first prayer, Tilano?
To go into the forest
And be content to sit
For many days alone,
Not asking God to come
Since He is present in the sun,
Simple and quiet in the tree and stone.

How many times have you watched the sun rise
That when I look into your eyes,
So old, so old and gay, I see there
That I have never learned the first prayer.

Plain grandeur escapes definition. You
Cannot speak about the mountains well.
About the clear plane, the sharp shadow
You cannot tell.

Mountains define you. You cannot define
Them. And all your looking serves to set
What you have learned of the stern line
Against an absolute.

The frail taut structure of a human face
Beside the sheer cliff drawn, all that you loved,
All that can stand in such a bare clear place
Is to be proved.

And love that is a landscape in the past
Becomes, like mountains, changeless. It is there.
It is standing against its own image at last
In a high air.

All day I had seen a nearer dot on the map, this town,
A night's sleep and the end of speeding and climbing
The steep magnificent hills, a way of coming home.

It is a still town where the past lies dreaming.

Drenched in the old sun, washed in the gold light,
Orderly and gay with white sills gleaming
And brick that glows by day and frames the night.

It is a warm town where the past is living.

The ancient walls draw comfort from the ancient trees.
Their roots are bound together in the earth and breathing.
They wear their double beauty with a marvelous ease.

It is a deep town where the past is sleeping,

And in the silence on the walks the soldiers' spurs
Are stilled and all the shouting and the women weeping
As the town is taken and lost in those unburied wars.

It is a strange town where the past is breathing.

For nothing is lost that has happened, nothing is over.
The traveller walking dark streets is silently leaving
His step beside Stonewall Jackson's like a lover—

For all foresees him here and he remembers all and knows
That from this past the future rises streaming,
And from this town relationship is born and flows.

It is a good town where the past is growing

Into the whole stretch of the land and touches all
With warmth about the heart and gives a form to living,
A still town where the stranger listens to his footsteps fall.

You cannot see them from the road: go far and deep,
Down the long avenues where mosses cover up the leaves,
Across the empty terraced lawns neglected and asleep,
To the still place where no dog barks and no dove grieves,
And a black mirror gives you back your face too white
In pools dyed jet by cypress roots: go deep and far,
Deep into time, far into crumbling spaces and half-light
To where they stand, our Egypt and our Nineveh.
Deep in a deathly stillness stand the planters' houses.

The garlands and the little foxes' faces carved
Upon the mantels look on empty walls and water-stains,
And the stairs tremble though so elegantly curved,
(Outside are waiting the bright creeping vines)
And as your foot falls in the silences, you guess
Decay has been arrested for a moment in the wall
But the grey plumes upon the trees in deathly loveliness
Will stir when you have passed, and somewhere a stone fall.
Deep in a deathly stillness stand the planters' houses.

There is no rice now and the world that sprang from it
Like an azalea, brilliant from the swamps, has crumbled.
A single century, it is embalmed as Egypt,
A single century, and all that elegance was humbled—
While we who fired that world and watched it burn
Come every spring to whisper near the tomb,
To stare, a little shaken, where the mosses mourn
And the azaleas and magnolias have not ceased to bloom.
Deep in a deathly stillness stand the planters' houses.

This legendary house, this dear enchanted tomb,
Once so supremely lived in, and for life designed,
Will none of mouldy death nor give it room,
Charged with the presence of a living mind.

Enter and touch the temper of a lively man.
See, it is spacious, intimate, and full of light.
The eye, pleased by detail, is nourished by the plan,
Nothing is here for show, much for delight.

All the joy of invention, and of craft and wit
Are freely granted here, all given rein,
But taut within the classic form and ruled by it,
Elegant, various, magnificent—and plain,

Europe become implacably American!
But Mozart still could have been happy here,
As Monroe riding from his farm again,
As well as any silversmith or carpenter—

As well as we, for whom this elegance,
This freedom in a form, this peaceful grace
Is not our heritage, although it happened once:
We read the future not the past upon his face.

"O Saisons! O Châteaux!"

Country of still canals, green willows, golden fields, all
Laid like a carpet for majestic winds to tread,
Where peace is in the lines of trees, but overhead
Heaven is marching: low lands where winds are tall,

Small lands where skies are the huge houses of the lark,
Rich lands where men are poor and reap what they have sown,
Who plant the small hugged acre where each works alone,
Men who rise with the sun and sleep with the early dark.

These are the country's marrow, these who work the land,
Passionate partisans and arguers but who still go on,
Whoever governs, planting the same seed under the same sun,
These who hold Flanders like a plough in the hand.

Their feet are rooted in earth but their hearts are moody,
Close to the dark skies, wind never still in their ears—
They were the battlefield of Europe for five hundred years.
The thunder may be guns. The skirts of the wind are bloody.

This land, this low land under threatening skies,
This Flanders full of skulls, has set a fury in the slow
Hearts of its people that, taking centuries to grow,
Now burns with a certain violence in their eyes.

It has made their land a passion which they must save
In every generation, spilling their blood to hold it.
Dogged and avaricious, they have never sold it.
Proud and fierce it has kept them. It has kept them brave.

Given their language coarseness, and a great breath
Of soldiers' laughter from the belly, and a flood
Of poetry that flows like war in the stream of their blood,
Slow and melancholy and half in love with death.

This was my father's country and the country of my birth,
And isn't it a strange thing that after the deliberate mind
Has yielded itself wholly to another land, stubborn and blind,
The heart gives its secret homage still to Flemish earth?

I knew it when I was seven, after the war and years of slumber,
The Flemish self awoke as we entered the Scheldt, and suddenly
The tears rushed to my eyes, though all we could see
Was a low land under a huge sky that did not remember.

Summer is all a green air—
From the brilliant lawn, sopranos
Through murmuring hedges
Accompanied by some poplars;
In fields of wheat, surprises;
Through faraway pastures, flows
To the horizon's blues
In slow decrescendos.

Summer is all a green sound—
Rippling in the foreground
To that soft applause,
The foam of Queen Anne's lace.
Green, green in the ear
Is all we care to hear.
Until a field suddenly flashes
The singing with so sharp
A yellow that it crashes
Loud cymbals in the ear.
Minor has turned to major
As summer, lulling and so mild,
Goes golden-buttercup-wild!

My eyes are full of rivers and trees tonight,
The clear waters sprung in the green,
The swan's neck flashing in sunlight,
The trees laced dark, the tiny unknown flowers,
Skies never still, shining and darkening the hours.
How can I tell you all that I have been?

My thoughts are rooted with the trees,
My thoughts flow with the stream.
They flow and are arrested as a frieze.
How can I answer now or tell my dream,
How tell you what is far and what is near?
Only that river, tree, and swan are here.

Even at the slow rising of the full moon,
That delicate disturber of the soul,
I am so drenched in rivers and in trees,
I cannot speak, I have nothing to tell,
Except that I must learn of this pure solitude
All that I am and might be, root and bone,
Flowing and still and beautiful and good,
Now I am almost earth and almost whole.

France like the map of tenderness fell open,
And green, green were the spreading arteries
Where every road was a double procession,
As poplar, maple, beech in leafy series
Opened the way to secret villages.
We were the wind, but even wind was slowed
As shadows made a river of the road.

We welcomed with a deep renewed devotion
Those gifts of evening wrapped in return:
The absent-minded cows moved in slow motion,
The sleeping dog did not stir at our horn,
The haycart stopped us, bulging at the barn,
And red geraniums on each window sill
Warmed like a handclasp, and as casual.

The immemorial boy fished in a stream
While the earth spun its way toward sleep;
Old women in the doorways sat to dream,
And at the fountain the old horse drank deep;
All animals and men were coming home.
We drove so fast it might have seemed like fleeing,
Yet all we knew was peace and its sweet flowing.

And as the moon rose and the mist rose too,
Still all we saw was radiance distilled
As we raced down the tree-roads into blue.
We were the new world nourished by the old,
The wild natural heart gravely fulfilled
By France at its most pure, that all men bless,
O human world, O map of tenderness!

The shadows are all black,
The sun intensely white,
And between this and that
No cloud or motion, but
Irradiating light.
Here silver olives shine
On terra cotta earth;
All scents are distilled—
Those fields of lavender
In the still, flaming air—
And sky so primary blue
The half-tones disappear,
Each color its most true,
Each object its most clear.

Here death does not come
Through rot or through decay.
There is no mould nor rust;
The stone falls to dust,
The face crumbles away
On the round portal,
While the still, burning dome,
Primary blue, stays on,
Unchanging and impartial.

Here the rich Roman arch
And high-pillared tomb
Where the winds play alone
And where no legions march,
Stands in its triumph plain
To be the shepherd's wonder.
Only the antique power
Has been slowly refined
By the long years of light
To a more human splendor—

Yet here no tears can fall;
Here there is nothing at all
Between death and desire,
Between earth and fire.

Here in the olive grove,
Under the cobalt dome,
The ancient spirits move
And light comes home,

And nests in silvery leaves.
It makes each branch a cloud,
And comes, and goes, and weaves
Aerial song aloud.

Here every branch is gifted
With spiritual fruit
And every leaf is lifted
To brightness from the root.

Where the terrestrial plane
Meets vision and desire,
The silver and the green
Are strung on a great lyre,

And leafy seraphim
The sun and shade among
Turn each grove to a hymn;
Whole hillsides are in song.

Silvery, shadowy now
The fruit over our head,
Who lie and hardly know
Which is light, which is bread.

Where waterfalls in shining folds
Trouble the classic pools,
And always formal green enfolds
And frames the moving grays and golds—
Who breathes on stone, who makes the rules?

The dazzling spray of fountains
And sunlight flashing these
Silver and gold suspensions
Broken by leaves—
Who plays with these subtle and gay dimensions?

The cold triumphant stairs
Gentled by lichen and old moss
Rise up from watery lairs
Where light and shadow cross—
Who is received at these grave receptions?

Who past the long wall saunters on
Down the cool sheltered paths alone,
And at last climbs the lichened stair
To stand, astonished, in a bright blue air?

It's Poetry, that's taken by surprise
In the most rigid of geometries.

ROMAN HEAD

First Century A.D.

An empire closing in
Clamps round the virile head,
As if he wore a crown,
As if the cropped hair weighed.

An open world of roads
Once branched out from his hand,
Now broken colonnades,
The arch sucked up by sand.

From those intense blank eyes
The intellect looks out
On nineteen centuries
And reads its own defeat.

This is the mortal head,
The fiery gloom on shade,
The master mastered
By the world he made.

This is the Roman head,
Riddled with self-despair,
By power corrupted—
The spirit fled to air,
The brittle glory fled.

We have come back to the cold North,
Come home after the passionate going forth,
After the olive groves, the Alpine meadow,
The purple seas under a mountain shadow,
The rich and crumbling ruins in the hills,
Those storms of light in the psychic cathedrals.
After the passionate summer going forth,
We have come back to the cold North.

We have come back at the year's turning,
Before the leaves fall, when the leaves are burning,
Before the apples, the late roses fall,
When all is empty and yet bountiful.
We have cried "Beauty, Beauty!" up and down,
But that restless pursuit is almost done,
And Beauty turned to ashes in the mouth,
Consumed by the consuming South.

Oh splendid was that spendthrift living,
The quick growth in the South, the over-giving,
But ripeness tumbles swiftly into ruin
And death is there under that awful sun,
The fig bursting with sweetness, the grape broken,
And every word too heavy that is spoken—
And we come back now, silenced, to this earth
To bind up selfhood in the North.

"O SAISONS! O CHÂTEAUX!"

When I landed it was coming home,
Home to all anguish, conflict and all love,
The heart stretched as the seasons move—
Summer is white roses and purple fox-glove,
Spring was a crimson tulip standing alone.
        We only keep what we lose.

O seasons, O castles, O splendor of trees!
The star of avenues and the triumphant square,
And in the Metro once a woman with red hair,
The weary oval face and tense France there,
Too few roots now, too many memories.
        We only keep what we lose.

The dark gloom of the forest and my dream,
The clouds that make the sky a tragic spell
And windows that frame partings in a well:
You bent down from a balcony to say farewell.
Across lost landscapes the trains scream.
        We only keep what we lose.

Parting freezes the image, roots the heart.
Once spring was a tulip standing alone,
Summer is a forest of roses and green.
No one will see again what I have seen.
And I possess you now from whom I part:
        We only keep what we lose.

I too have known the inward disturbance of exile,
The great peril of being at home nowhere,
The dispersed center, the dividing love,
Not here, nor there, leaping across ocean,
Turning, returning to each strong allegiance,
American, but with this difference, parting.

Wherever I could be was always parting,
Always anxiety, the sense of exile,
Settled in no place but a frightening nowhere.
And yet how strong was the transplanted love
Thrusting a fierce root into earth from ocean,
Seeking the nourishment of old allegiance.

Later the mind, Protean in allegiance,
Uprooted though it was, soon after parting
Did flower suddenly, astonished in its exile,
Became accustomed to a rootless nowhere,
Quick to bear fruit, but Oh my busy love
Needed those numbing journeys across ocean,

Made memory magic in the lapse of ocean,
Rehearsed the ancient cities till allegiance
Became eternal meeting and eternal parting,
A beautiful malaise between worlds of exile.
Would there be somewhere, someday instead of nowhere,
A rock-bed for the elastic quickened love?

Can world-divisions heal a haunted love,
Now all earth is transformed to treacherous ocean?
What continent can hold our whole allegiance?
The whole world weeps, and there's an end of parting.
The tears of men are all the tears of exile.
Was it no place then, language, nightmare nowhere

But failure to recognize that Hell is nowhere
And becomes somewhere only through our love?

Insight by anguish fired leaps across ocean;
There are no formulas for this allegiance.
I've had to push on to the end of parting,
To emerge clumsily from inward exile,

Try to come home to a place beyond exile
Where love, that airy tree, is separate nowhere,
Greening impartial, over every parting.

The Action of The Beautiful

Here in two ways perspective leads us on
From matter and from moment: we explore
A flight of arches diminished one by one
Above converging lines upon the floor;
They bring us, captivated, to an open door.

From everything that might trouble the mind
This narrowing path is drawn to set us free,
Sends us to Heaven curiously designed—
We cannot help but go there when we see
The hill, the cool blue air, the pointed tree.

The matter and the moment are forgotten
But they are always there, still taking place.
The angel tells of Love to be begotten,
And we, who have been running free in space,
Come back, refreshed, to meet it face to face.

Granted this world is an imagined one,
Existing in the mind, only the mind,
And it will vanish in the actual sun,
Having no power to turn the clear eye blind.

A cool glass country where the heavy green
Fruit hangs untouchable, transparent,
Flowers not to be touched but only seen:
Nothing is real yet everything apparent.

Here we have come believing the desire
To break a flower is a dream of the hand
To which it cannot in reality aspire—
Where petals are of glass, you understand.

And yet we move, are without question moving,
Out of this room, this chair, this certain hour
To that imagined country, the fruit-loving,
Where the hand shatters the glass flower,

The moment when the unbeliever sees
The warm blood trickle on the actual wrist,
Where the imagined orchard of glass trees
Yields flower and fruit into the wounded fist

Though he must wake to find it as before,
Himself still sitting in that room, that chair,
No shattered crystal fruit upon the floor,
No treasure in his hand that was not there.

Granted this world is an imagined place
(Real and unreal are easily divisible)
But what then of the anguish on his face?
The wound is there although invisible.

The fruit is picked, broken the glassy rind,
The flower on the floor and shattered,
Though it existed only in the mind,
This orchard—though it never mattered.

I move through my world like a stranger
Where multiple images collide and fall,
Fragments of eyes, lakes—or a mirror.
How to include, make peace with them all?

Only your face (is this too illusion?)
So poised between silence and speech
Suggests that at the center of confusion
An inward music is just within reach.

Can so much be spoken by an eyelid,
Or the bent forehead so much light distill?
Here all is secret and yet nothing hid,
That tenderness, those deep reserves of will.

There is no future, past, only pure presence.
The moment of a glance is brimmed so full
It fuses consciousness to a new balance:
This is the action of the beautiful.

Lakes, mirrors, every broken radiance
Shine whole again in your reflective face,
And I, the stranger, centered in your presence,
Come home and walk into the heart of peace.

We enter this evening as we enter a quartet
Listening again for its particular note,
The interval when all seems possible,
Order within time when action is suspended
And we are pure in heart, perfect in will.
We enter the evening whole and well-defended
But at the quick of self, intense detachment
That is a point of burning far from passion—
And this, we know, is what we always meant
And even love must learn it in some fashion,
To move like formal music through the heart,
To be achieved like some high difficult art.

We enter the evening as we enter a quartet
Listening again for its particular note
Which is your note, perhaps, your special gift,
A detached joy that flowers and makes bloom
The longest silence in the silent room—
And there would be no music if you left.

The Cluny Tapestries

I am the unicorn and bow my head
You are the lady woven into history
And here forever we are bound in mystery
Our wine, Imagination, and our bread,
And I the unicorn who bows his head.

You are all interwoven in my history
And you and I have been most strangely wed
I am the unicorn and bow my head
And lay my wildness down upon your knee
You are the lady woven into history.

And here forever we are sweetly wed
With flowers and rabbits in the tapestry
You are the lady woven into history
Imagination is our bridal bed:
We lie ghostly upon it, no word said.

Among the flowers of the tapestry
I am the unicorn and by your bed
Come gently, gently to bow down my head,
Lay at your side this love, this mystery,
And call you lady of my tapestry.

I am the unicorn and bow my head
To one so sweetly lost, so strangely wed:

You sit forever under a small formal tree
Where I forever search your eyes to be

Rewarded with this shining of our tragedy
And know your beauty was not cast for me,

Know we are woven all in mystery,
The wound imagined where no one has bled,

My wild love chastened to this history
Where I, before your eyes, bow down my head.

This is the love I bring,
Absolute and nothing:
A tree but with no root,
A cloud heavy with fruit,
A wide stone stair
That leads nowhere
But to empty sky,
Ambiguous majesty.

This is the love I bear:
It is light as air,
Yet weighs like the earth;
It is water flowing,
Yet adamant as fire.
It is coming from going.
It is dying and growing.

A love so rare and hard
It cuts a diamond word
Upon the windowpane,
"Never, never again,
Never upon my breast,"
Having no time to bring,
Having no place to rest,
Absolute and nothing.

1

It was late in September when you took me
To that amazing garden, hidden in the city,
Tranquil and complicated as an open hand,
There among green pleasances and descant of fountains,
Through walled paths and dappled loggias
Opening to distant trees,
We went conversing, smoking, often silent,
Our feet cool in sandals, nonchalant as the air.

It was at the end of September, warm for the season.
Nothing had fallen yet to bruise the grass.
Ripeness was all suspended,
The air aromatic and fresh over sun-drenched box.

Critical as Chinese philosophers,
We performed the garden by easy stages:
Should we move toward shade or toward sunlight,
The closed dark pool or the panoplied fountain?
Clearly each path had a metaphysical meaning,
Those rustic steps, that marble balustrade.
It was late in September when time,
Time that is not ours,
Hid itself away.

2

Our first arrival was a square room,
Brilliant parquet of clover
Designed as a stage for the trees
And their subtle conversations,
Diapason of faintly stirring leaves;
The fountains, heard not seen,
Made silence crepitant and watery.
And here it seemed we were part of a discourse
On the ancient themes,
Perspective and enclosure,

Desire raised and fulfilled
To this complex alive composure.

It was there that your voice,
Harsh and aloof,
Mixed with the cry of a bird
As a cardinal flashed through the willow
And screamed.

3

We climbed lightly
Through a small steep orchard
To a bastion of branches.
Must we penetrate, force passage
At the top of the hill?
No airy place, no view?

What we found was a grave high room,
Lonely, enclosed in acacias,
Its center a double pool
Where ivy crept and crowded
And water lilies slept, going to seed.
We had not after all expected
A place so perfectly round.
We sat on a stone bench like statues.
Nothing moved.

Nothing moved for a long season.
From high in the sunlight, then
A single leaf fell slowly,
And we watched it fall.
So passionate was the place, so still,
This light leaf falling from air to grass
Was monumental. It held
The exact weight of a tremendous word.

How gentle and relieving
Then to emerge, climb down
From that intense enclosure
High on the hill
To the large view we had imagined
Through all the devious paths,
The orchards, loggias,
The long boxed-in perspectives.

Now it was here,
The weight of the trees flung back,
The undulating ample slopes,
The whole shape of the land
Made clear in the golden light.
In the foreground tawny dogwood
Thick with vermilion berries, showed
Brilliantly sharp.
We could read each leaf.

We had to climb down
To get to contemplation
On this scale, large, airy, remote.
We sat on a homely wooden bench
And watched a solitary gardener pass
With his pruning hook.
Indeed it was coming home
To an unbroken sunlit peace of knowing.

The Sacred Wood

Sometimes it seems to be the inmost land
All children still inhabit when alone.
They play the game of morning without end,
And only lunch can bring them, startled, home
Bearing in triumph a small speckled stone.

Yet even for them, too much dispersal scatters;
What complex form the simplest game may hold!
And all we know of time that really matters
We've learned from moving clouds and waters
Where we see form and motion lightly meld.

Not the fixed rigid object, clock or mind,
But the long ripple that opens out beyond
The duck as he swims down the tranquil pond,
Or when a wandering, falling leaf may find
And follow the formal downpath of the wind.

It is, perhaps, our most complex creation,
A lovely skill we spend a lifetime learning,
Something between the world of pure sensation
And the world of pure thought, a new relation,
As if we held in balance the globe turning.

Even a year's not long, yet moments are.
This moment, yours and mine, and always given,
When the leaf falls, the ripple opens far,
And we go where all animals and children are,
The world is open. Love can breathe again.

SUN BOAT

As if this light boat had no keel,
As if the mast carried no sail,
With no hand on the tiller to guide
The gentle rocking, the glide,

It swings up, floated on air,
And no changeable wind there,
Only the lightest little motion,
That ripple on the pulse of ocean,

As the sun breathes in stillness, weaves
The warmth in slowly rising waves.
And if the boat seems strangely gifted,
It is that it is being lifted.

The mariner has yielded will
And given to the sun his skill,
And lost his course in summer air
Content to be a passenger.

At the bottom of the green field she lies,
Abandoned foreground to the rooted trees,
To the house and children; in her open eyes
The birds' wings flash; there is a hum of bees
In the air overhead, in the flowers of the lime.
She is a plant. Without words, she speaks;
Without moving, grows; lives without time.
Has she been there for days, perhaps for weeks?

At the bottom of the green field she lies,
Without moving, moves. She becomes a stream.
Clouds pass in and out of her open eyes
And no one knows the content of this dream.
She has become a source, mysterious flow
That is forever rooted, and yet passes,
The ripple of silence infinitely slow.
She lies as if asleep down in the grasses.

When will the diviner be sent for to strike
The hidden source with his wand and there the wand
Leap up out of his hands as the waters wake,
She wake from her dream, alive and stunned,
The heart shape transparent in her breast,
And listen to its voice, buried so deep,
She does not hear, nor know how far from sleep,
How far this intense growth is from rest.

At the bottom of the green field she lies,
Deep in the spring, lost in its mysteries.

I thought of happiness, how it is woven
Out of the silence in the empty house each day
And how it is not sudden and it is not given
But is creation itself like the growth of a tree.
No one has seen it happen, but inside the bark
Another circle is growing in the expanding ring.
No one has heard the root go deeper in the dark,
But the tree is lifted by this inward work
And its plumes shine, and its leaves are glittering.

So happiness is woven out of the peace of hours
And strikes its roots deep in the house alone:
The old chest in the corner, cool waxed floors,
White curtains softly and continually blown
As the free air moves quietly about the room;
A shelf of books, a table, and the white-washed wall—
These are the dear familiar gods of home,
And here the work of faith can best be done,
The growing tree is green and musical.

For what is happiness but growth in peace,
The timeless sense of time when furniture
Has stood a lifespan in a single place,
And as the air moves, so the old dreams stir
The shining leaves of present happiness?
No one has heard thought or listened to a mind,
But where people have lived in inwardness
The air is charged with blessing and does bless;
Windows look out on mountains and the walls are kind.

In this land, Rilke's country if you will,
Nothing is closed or intact.
The mountains open out an airy world and spill
Height as an ethos. We live in the vertical.
Angels, often invoked, become a fact.

And they have names, Cloud, Stone, Sun, Vine,
But the names are interchangeable.
All meld together in making the same flowing design;
We drink conjunction in the mingled wine.
The journey is infinite and it is immobile.

This is what he found after all the busy wanderings,
This childhood dream of a lonely tower
Set in a mountain-meadow world where the air sings
And the names are interchangeable of cloud and flower.
This is what he found: the grass full of springs.

A sacramental earth; reality both stalked
And made the vision clear.
And here the living waters sprang up where he walked.
It was the clouds and not himself who talked.
Was he the ghost who felt himself so near?

At Muzot he stood at last at the intersection
Of God and self (nothing is closed).
The voice he heard came from dissolving stone.
Even the mountains ascended and were gone,
And he himself stood naked and disclosed.

There by the waterfall
In the dappled green light
By the shaggy white coat
Of the steep fall, in a second
Dream and reality were wedded.

The boy glimmered
Among the hollowed darkness of the rocks,
Shot through the shallow places laughing,
Stood in the sunlight, high up,
And, like a god suspended in green air,
He followed falling water and downstruck
Deep in the round pool. It trembled
With the force of that arrow in it.

What the mind pondered,
What the eye saw, met and
Were suddenly connected,
Opened the world within
As spirit sprang to sunlight.

Boy, did you meet Sabrina? Was she there?

To probe the secret dappled pools, to find her
Clothed in the curling sheepskin of the foam,
Under the green wave smiling, mind must be a diver.
It must follow the waters and take to the air.

Boy, dive again!
Suspended for a second in green air.
Perform and save us.
                    But there is only silence.

There is no connection any more between the pool
And the boy, between the actual image and the vision.
Dream and reality are parted.
                    There is only, without end, division.

A charm of columns crowds
The tranquil glade;
No leaves to be seen,
The sudden rush of green
Makes of the air a cloud
Above the colonnade.

And this perspective breathes;
Unchanging, yet it grows.
The rich lives of the trees
Renew through centuries
Those columns and those wreaths
Through which the season flows.

The green rush comes and goes,
Light bursting through stained glass;
The coppers shine and fall
In the great airy hall,
But winter only shows
Structure more marvelous—

The columns in a choir
Define the empty air;
That leafy cloud has gone
But only to bring on
This magic more severe,
The crucial form laid bare.

Oh answer to a prayer
And to an old long hunger,
This ancient fertile glade,
This living colonnade
Where form and content are
Not parted any longer!

LIFTING STONE

A painting by Katharine Sturgis

This is an ancient scene: we stand and stare
As hills are excavated and then lifted;
Swung on the cable's perpendicular,
The load is pivotal to earth and air,
A feather-balance, and so delicate
The stone floats up as if it had no weight.

Below, a solitary figure stands
To gentle the long bundle from its bed;
Athens and Troy are leaning from his hands;
The Roman arch, then perilous Chartres ascends
Out of the empty spacious world where he
Nudges rich burdens toward history.

Who with his own machineries of skill
Has not dreamed often of this very place?
Painter and poet lift the buried hill
To build a pyramid or clean bright wall,
And the great spires that sleep in this quarry
Are excavated toward the clouds they marry.

What soars is always buried deep for ages,
Gently explored in the hill's dark mind,
Prized, hewn in slow thoughtful stages,
Then floated on these airy equipages,
Watched by a figure standing there alone
Whose work, humble and hard, is lifting stone.

Leaves Before The Wind

THE SWANS

I think this was a dream and yet we saw
The low stone bridge, the still canal,
And I remember how laburnum threw
A gold rain on the water very well—
After all, what we saw may have been true.

There in a rocky angle the two swans
On a small platform fashioned like a stage
In all that watery world were rooted ones,
And face to face the snowy double image
Stood entranced there among the ancient stones.

Then, as we watched, the ritual play began;
They arched their wings full-span and shivered once,
Then gravely bowed their heads and, swan to swan,
Lifted their heavy bodies in the dance,
Their long necks sinuous upon the silence,

Their long necks writing figures on the air
As if, like skates on ice, their beaks must draw
A precise pattern, and what was written there,
Repeated with a concentrated awe,
Until the tension seemed too great to bear.

In one ecstatic motion, straight and pure,
The weaving necks were lifted, and each now
Stretched to the sky as if he could endure
The little space between them better so,
And trembled. How immaculate they were!

Who would not pray, looking at such a scene,
To be alive, passionate, part of the dance,
And gladly yielding up all that is human,
A part of natural delight for once,
Lovers take on the grave shape of the swan?

How pure the hearts of lovers as they walk
Through the rich quiet fields
Where the stiff wheat grows heavy on the stalk,
And over barley and its paler golds,
The air is bright—

Would touch it all, embrace, learn it by hand,
Plunging their faces into the thick grain,
To stroke as well see the cow's soft flank,
To feel the beech trunk harsh under the palm,
And oh, to drink the light!

They do not even walk yet hand in hand,
But every sense is pricked alive so sharp
That life breathes through them from the burning land,
And they could use the wind itself for harp,
And pluck the vibrant green.

At first the whole world opens into sense:
They learn their love by looking at the wheat,
And there let fall all that was shy and tense
To walk the season slowly on propitious feet,
And be all they have seen.

While all around them earth moves toward an end,
The gold turning to bronze, the barley tasselled,
Where the great sheaves will be stored up and bend
Their heads together in that rich wedding bed
All are about to enter.

The hearts of lovers as they walk, how pure;
How cool the wind upon the open palm
As they move on toward harvest, and so sure
Even this ripening has a marvelous calm
And a still center.

We have walked, looking at the actual trees:
The chestnut leaves wide-open like a hand,
The beech leaves bronzing under every breeze,
We have felt flowing through our knees
  As if we were the wind.

We have sat silent when two horses came,
Jangling their harness, to mow the long grass.
We have sat long and never found a name
For this suspension in the heart of flame
  That does not pass.

We have said nothing; we have parted often,
Not looking back, as if departure took
An absolute of will—once not again.
(But this is each day's feat, as when
  The heart first shook.)

Where fervor opens every instant so,
There is no instant that is not a curve,
And we are always coming as we go;
We lean toward the meeting that will show
  Love's very nerve.

And so exposed (O leaves before the wind!)
We bear this flowing fire, forever free,
And learn through devious paths to find
The whole, the center, and perhaps unbind
  The mystery

Where there are no roots, only fervent leaves,
Nourished on meditations and the air,
Where all that comes is also all that leaves,
And every hope compassionately lives
  Close to despair.

We saw the rich leaves turning brown
And the small perfect grapes go sour,
Wizened by the devouring sun;
The brazen sky without a saving cloud
Burned on with an implacable blue fire,
And we were parched and dying like the vine
And only prayed to see the sun go down.

Until at last—after what nights of fever
When a full moon glittered the dead sky—
We saw the weighted clouds come slowly over,
Purple, tumultuous against the brassy blue,
To burst upon the arid heights in thunder,
And our hearts like wild horses plunged,
Chaotic, trembling, in an agony of weather.

But when the rush of rain in mercy fell,
We knew the healing in our very bones,
And all the suffering landscape was made well:
Love rises green among the burning stones
Now that the little wizened grapes can swell.

Measure force of tension
By its end,
From the strained suspension
Supported, spanned
On taut skies of will
Slack now, sudden, and
Heavily we fall.

Mortal is the tug
Of gravity,
And the heart-huge hug
That pulls down sky.
Dark clouds enfold us
And then fall away—
Nothing to hold us.

Toward what landing
Do we fast-fall
In this strange unhanding
And release of will,
Heavy bodies now
(Sky, farewell!)
To what earth below?

Toward a new land,
But from where or why
Never understand,
Who you are or I,
What perils and what charms
Come by chance to lie
In each other's arms.

Now voyager, lay here your dazzled head.
Come back to earth from air, be nourishèd,
Not with that light on light, but with this bread.

Here close to earth be cherished, mortal heart,
Hold your way deep as roots push rocks apart
To bring the spurt of green up from the dark.

Where music thundered let the mind be still,
Where the will triumphed let there be no will,
What light revealed, now let the dark fulfill.

Here close to earth the deeper pulse is stirred,
Here where no wings rush and no sudden bird,
But only heart-beat upon beat is heard.

Here let the fiery burden be all spilled,
The passionate voice at last be calmed and stilled
And the long yearning of the blood fulfilled.

Now voyager, come home, come home to rest,
Here on the long-lost country of earth's breast
Lay down the fiery vision, and be blest, be blest.

Indeed I loved these hands and knew them well—
Nervous, expressive, holding a Chinese pink,
A child, a book, always withdrawn and still
As if they had it in their power to think,
Hands that the Flemish masters have explored,
Who gave delicate strength and mystic grace
To contemplative men, to women most adored
As if to give the inmost heart a face—
Indeed I learned to love these secret hands
Before I found them here, open to mine,
And clasped the mystery no one understands,
Read reverence in their five-fold design,
Where animals and children may be healed
And in the slightest gesture Love revealed.

Beautiful is this day that brings us home
From our domain of cold and winter bower,
From iron earth to trees in tasselly flower,
And gentle airs, and the soft-springing loam.

Offhand and royal, we are the carefree lords
Of these sumptuous rooms where light flows green,
These corridors of air, these feathery swards
Under a sky-blue ceiling, high and clean.

We lie on an enormous grassy bed
Sheltered as princes under the mothering air,
Where the anemone shines like a star,
And rivers flow through veined leaves overhead;

And hold each other close in the green chance,
Hold each other against time and waste,
Come home here in a spring that is only once,
And watch how the birds are swift, yet without haste.

At last we inhabit the dream, are really floating
As princes of the hour, while these green palaces
Glide into summer, where we too are going
With all the birds, and leaves, and all the kisses.

Locked to each other's heart, floating at rest,
These lovers stream the night like constellations,
The throat a flaming pillar and the breast
A Milky Way, these shining convocations
In one brief hour reverse the elements,
And bring down to the earth the starry sky;
A single touch haloes the shadowy hands,
And brilliant as the Pleiades they lie,
Floating like milkweed on the winter cold,
Resting as gently on the weightless air;
They will not ever change, will not grow old,
Who have flown out of time and wander there
In radiance that's counted in light-years—
Until dawn tilts earth back: a tree appears.

For a time it is part of the machinery
Of feeling, one of the several counters
In the game: romantic love encounters
Death and death is romantic scenery,
A stage-device for deepening the view,
Papier-maché of course. It can't be true.

Later it will become the central fact,
Not in imagination's realm at all,
But reckoned with, an implacable fall,
And to be felt under each wish or act—
The kiss straight from the terrible heart
That will not beat forever must, does hurt.

Death becomes real, and love is forced to grow;
These lovers do not turn away to weep,
But hold carefully all they have to keep,
And stare long at all they have to know.
When every gesture is made upon a quicksand
Touch must be absolute, and firm the hand.

Not by not seeing, but by seeing through:
With fresh clear eyes they search out each other
As once the infant searched to find the mother
And make a strong one out of a frail two.
These lovers who have learned to reckon death
Are lightly married on the moment's breath.

1

These images remain, these classic landscapes
That lie immense and quiet behind eyes
Enlarged by love to think only in shapes
That compass time and frame the changing skies,
Triumph of arch, of spire, triumph of trees,
The pure perspective, the poignant formal scene.
Pursued by time, still we were given these.
Even the flames of spring were frozen green,
Fountains suspended crystal in the air
And every open square could make us glad.
Where we stood once, once free to stand and stare
Imagination wanders like a god.
These images exist. They have not changed,
Though we are caught by time, by time estranged.

2

The stone withstands: the chisel does destroy.
But out of deprivation the grave image
Slowly emerges, and the sculptor's joy
Is made out of a self-denying rage—
Cut down and cast away, break to the core.
Whatever easy triumph falls in chips
And lies dispersed in waste upon the floor
He gladly yields for the sake of those lips,
That savage throat that opens the whole chest,
Tension so great between him and the stone,
It seems he carries vengeance in his wrist.
Now take the chisel and make for the bone!
Difficult love, you are the sculptor here,
The image you must wrest, great and severe.

3

What angel can I leave, gentle and stern,
What healing presence to be to you at last
The journey's end, the absolute return,
The future bringing gifts out of the past?
What angel can I take, gentle and pure,
To make of absence an open place of joy,
Now the perspective grows in depth, mature
Untroubled love no parting can destroy,
As a great formal square where centuries
Only enrich the earlier design,
And cast a deeper shadow from the frieze
Of later leaves, and clarify the line.
The angel of these spaces as we part
Opens the sleeping city of the heart.

4

Here are the peaceful days we never knew.
Here are the leaves. Here are the silent flowers,
And you are reading poems while I sew.
The hours are light. We do not count the hours.
There is no need of words. Our lives will do,
Long long enough to learn all of our love,
While time, the river, flows gently below,
Having no false eternities to prove.
The night is full of unspent tenderness
And in its silences we rest apart.
There is no need of words with which to bless
The daily bread, the wine of the full heart.
Here are the peaceful days we cannot share.
Here is our peace at last, and we not there.

5

But parting is return, the coming home,
Parting in space and yet the dearest meeting,
Where we most seem to go, there most do come
And give each other an eternal greeting,
Love is restored to nobleness and peace,
Rooted in reason as abstract and pure
As the equation where all questions cease,
Love with its deepest meaning to endure,
Endure and grow through all anxiety,
Until when standing on the very quicksand
Passion itself finds roots again in pity;
We take each other gently by the hand,
In deeper need demanding deeper union,
Parting become arrival and communion.

Consider the mysterious salt:
In water it must disappear.
It has no self. It knows no fault.
Not even sight may apprehend it.
No one may gather it or spend it.
It is dissolved and everywhere.

But out of water into air
It must resolve into a presence,
Precise and tangible and here.
Faultlessly pure, faultlessly white,
It crystallizes in our sight
And has defined itself to essence.

What element dissolves the soul
So it may be both found and lost,
In what suspended as a whole?
What is the element so blest
That there identity can rest
As salt in the clear water cast?

Love in its early transformation,
And only love, may so design it
That the self flows in pure sensation,
Is all dissolved and found at last
Without a future or a past,
And a whole life suspended in it.

The faultless crystal of detachment
Comes after, cannot be created
Without the first intense attachment.
Even the saints achieve this slowly;
For us, more human and less holy,
In time like air is essence stated.

Binding The Dragon

Pain can make a whole winter bright,
Like fever force us to live deep and hard,
Betrayal focus in a peculiar light
All we have ever dreamed or known or heard,
And from great shocks we do recover.
Like Wright's hotel, we seem to have been fashioned
To take earthquake and stand upright still.
Alive among the wreckage we discover
Death or ruin is not less impassioned
Than we ourselves, and not less terrible,
Since we nicely absorb and can use them all.

It is the small shock, hardly noticed
At the time, the slight increase in gloom,
Daily attrition loosening the fist,
The empty mailbox in the afternoon,
The loss of memory, the gradual weakening
Of fiery will, defiant to exist,
That slowly undermines the solid walls,
Until the building that withstood an earthquake
Falls clumsily among the usual days.
Our last courage has been subtly shaken:
When the cat dies, we are overtaken.

One is large and lazy;
One is old and crazy;
One is young and witty;
One is a great beauty,
But all feed you the wind,
And each of them is blind.

How then to recognize
The hard unseeing eyes,
Or woman tell from ghost?
Human each is, almost—
That wild and glittering light—
Almost, and yet not quite.

Never look straight at one
For then your pride is gone.
The empty eyes give back
Your own most bitter lack,
And what they have to tell
Is your most secret Hell:

The old, the sad pursuit
Of the corrupting fruit,
The slightly tainted dish
Of the subconscious wish,
Fame, love, or merely pride
Exacerbate, provide.

Wrap you in glamour cold,
Warm you with fairy gold,
Till you grow fond and lazy,
Witty, perverse, and crazy,
And drink their health in wind,
And call the Furies kind.

"The dragon's Proteus. He must be fought,
And fighting dragons is my holy joy,"
The poet says, although he may look caught
And blood is spurting from one eye.

"Sublimate," says the cautious analyst.
The poet answers, "Let him do it first.
Look, I have got this dragon in my fist.
I'll hold him there until he dies of thirst."

But suddenly the dragon flows away.
The dragon is a river: you can't do it,
Hold up a river in your hands all day.
"And what is sublimation?" asks the poet.

"Is it to translate water into fire?
Is it to follow birds along the air?
Is it to be the master of desire,
Or ride a cycle with no handlebar?

Gentle a dragon to lie quiet there,
Beautiful in his power but asleep,
Image of dragon resting on the air?"
The poet asked, and then began to weep.

He did not want the dragon to be caught.
He wanted it alive and in his fist.
For who would kill the god with whom he fought?
And so he wept and cursed the analyst.

The frog, that naked creature,
Arouses immediate pity;
He does not burst except in fables, but
He looks as if he might,
So violent his anxiety,
So exposed his nature.
His brilliant eyes look wildly out
As if the pulse were leaping from his throat.

We feel his being more, now
We have grown so vulnerable,
Have become so wholly exposed with the years
To primeval powers;
These storms are often terrible,
Followed by sudden snow.
It is alarming to feel the soul
Leap to the surface and find no sheltering wall.

Is this growth, we wonder?
But it makes us tremble
Because we are not able to conceal
The rage, the fear we feel,
Nor able to dissemble
Those claps of thunder
When we are seized and shaken beyond our will
By the secret demon or the secret angel.

To show the very pulse
Of thought alive,
Transparent as the frog whose every mood
Glows through his cold red blood—
For whom we grieve
Because he has no walls—
Giving up pride, to endure shame and pity,
Is this a valid choice, choice of maturity?

It is time the big bird with the angry neck
We have cajoled and cursed
Went home to die, or whatever he must do
When his heart would burst.

For his wild desire pulses over our heads
And opens the secret night,
Passage of wings that madden without release
When the phoenix is in flight.

Let him go, stretching his long legs, clumsy
On this harsh ground. Let him flee
To the soft black marshes he remembers
Or the gentle mother tree.

Let him go. He has shaken the house at night;
His wings have clouded our dream.
And there is no peace for his lost cry at daybreak
And at night his terrible scream.

He flames through the morning yet he never sings;
He only makes that strange lost cry.
He is angry all the time. Let him find his tree
And make his nest and die.

Though he is God's own angel in disguise,
We cannot bear another angry word,
Nor look into those cold and jewelled eyes,
O pitiless strange bird!

Will he come back, will he come back all shining
From his dark death to bring
The true message, the gentle, that all his torment
Was desperate to sing?

Or—what if it were not he at all, not he
Who must consume himself to be reborn,
But we ourselves who drove an angel from us
Because our hearts were torn?

O joie—mon abîme parle. J'ai retourné
vers la lumière ma dernière profondeur!
—Nietzsche

These were her nightly journeys made alone,
The prisoner of seas which cannot drown,
Forced to descend the vertical
Plunges of dream.
Though all day long she knew no fear would come
And freely walked (who once in dreams had flown)
At night, she fell.
Burdens returned to magnetize the bone,
And in her helpless sleep she was hurled down.

Waters were heavy round her; she was bound
To heaviness of falling, falling with no end,
Imprisoned plunge
Sucked by dense air;
Or, worse, vertiginous oceans with no floor.
She fell and must keep falling, nearly drowned,
Yet cling to the lunge,
Gasp for more breath, for falling must extend:
She would be dead if once she touched the ground.

Yet once on that voyage through the night, she was
Given (but how? but why?) the means of choice:
She might choose to ascend
The falling dream,
By some angelic power without a name
Reverse the motion, plunge into upwardness,
Know height without an end,
Density melt to air, silence yield a voice—
Within her fall she felt the pull of Grace.

Through the descending motion a strong thrust
Strengthened her upward against the fluid wall,
So splitting-fierce a tension,
Psychic strain,

She turned weak, dizzy for downwardness again,
But was upheld, drawn upward, upward to free air,
Felt herself all ascension,
And, floating through blue spaces over all,
Needed no walls, suspended on pure trust.

And when she came back to cool daylight, found
That she brought with her from that mystic sleep
The saving true event,
The image raised
In glass at a great height where angels blazed,
And there, at Chartres, as the sun made its round,
One crimson angel sent
A bolt down to her human world to keep,
A bolt that struck her knees back to the ground,

A bolt that raised her heart to blazing height
And made the vertical the very thrust of hope,
And found its path at last
(Slow work of Grace)
Into the texture of the nightmare place,
Shot through the falling dream, entered her night,
Lifted her past
The watery dark burdens, the descending slope
Until she was both grounded, and in flight.

Not to rebel against what pulls us down,
The private burdens each of us could name
That weigh heavily in the blood and bone
So that we stumble, clumsy half the time,
Unable to love well or love at all.
Who knows the full weight that another bears,
What obscure densities sustains alone,
To burst fearfully through what self-locked doors?
So heavy is our walk with what we feel,
And cannot tell, and cannot ever tell.

Oh, to have the lightness, the savoir faire
Of a tightrope walker, his quicksilver tread
As he runs softly over the taut steel thread;
Sharp as a knifeblade cutting walls of air,
He's pitted against weights we cannot see,
All tension balanced, though we see him only
A rapture of grace and skill, focussed and lonely.

Is it a question of discipline or grace?
The steel trap of the will or some slight shift
Within an opened consciousness?
The tightrope walker juggles weights to lift
Himself up on the stress, and, airy master
Of his own loss, he springs from heaviness.
But we, stumbling our way, how learn such poise,
The perfect balance of all griefs and joys?
Burdened by love, how learn the light release
That out of stress, can somersault to peace?

Vision is locked in stone.
The lion in the air is gone
With the great lion of the sun.
The sky is wild and cold.
The tawny fire is gone.
The hill where love did open like a rose
Is black. It snows.

Emptiness flows.
The flowers in the heart all close
Drowned in a heavy white. Love knows
That poverty untold,
The cave where nothing grows.
The flaming lions of the flesh are gone,
Their power withdrawn.

God of the empty room,
Thy will be done. Thy will be done.
Now shine the inward sun,
The beating heart that glows
Within the skeleton,
The magic rose, the purer living gold,
Shine now, grown old.

All that is young and bold,
The lion's roar, the flaming skin and wild,
Unearthly peace now cherish and enfold
And fresh sleep overcome,
That in this death-in-life, delicate, cold,
The spiritual rose
Flower among the snows—

The love surpassing love.

On a winter night
I sat alone
In a cold room,
Feeling old, strange
At the year's change
In fire light.

Last fire of youth,
All brilliance burning
And my year turning,
One dazzling rush
Like a wild wish
Or blaze of truth.

First fire of age
And the soft snow
Of ash below—
For the clean wood
The end was good.
For me, an image.

For then I saw
That fires, not I,
Burn down and die;
That flare of gold
Turns old, turns cold.
Not I. I grow.

Nor old, nor young,
The burning sprite
Of my delight,
A salamander
In fires of wonder,
Gives tongue, gives tongue!

Now I become myself. It's taken
Time, many years and places;
I have been dissolved and shaken,
Worn other people's faces,
Run madly as if Time were there
Terribly old, crying a warning,
"Hurry, you will be dead before—"
(What? Before you reach the morning?
Or the end of the poem is clear?
Or love safe in the walled city?)
Now to stand still, to be here,
Feel my own weight and density.
The black shadow on the paper
Is my hand; the shadow of a word,
As thought shapes the shaper,
Falls heavy on the page, is heard.
All fuses now, falls into place
From wish to action, word to silence,
My work, my love, my time, my face
Gathered into one intense
Gesture of growing like a plant.
As slowly as the ripening fruit
Fertile, detached, and always spent,
Falls but does not exhaust the root,
So all the poem is, can give
Grows in me to become the song,
Made so and rooted so by love.
Now there is time and Time is young.
O, in this single hour I live
All of myself and do not move.
I, the pursued, who madly ran,
Stand still, stand still, and stop the sun!

All Souls

(In Memoriam, E.M.S.)

Though in a little while
You will be dead again
After this first rehearsal
Since then and all the pain,
Still it's not death that spends
So tenderly this treasure
In leaf-rich golden winds,
But life in lavish measure.

October spends the aster,
Riches of purple, blue,
Lavender, white that glow
In ragged starry cluster.
Then when November comes,
Shaggy chrysanthemums,
Salmon-pink, saffron-yellow,
All coppers bright and mellow,
Stand up against the frost
And never count the cost.

No, it's not death this year
Since then and all the pain.
It's life we harvest here
(Sun on the crimson vine).
The garden speaks your name.
We drink your joys like wine.

How to lay down her death,
Bring her back living
Into the open heart, the over-grieving,
Bury once and for all the starving breath,
And lay down her death?

Not on love's breast
Lay down this heavy prize
And close at last the open, the gray eyes
Of her who in my woe can find no rest—
Not on love's breast.

And not in solitude
Lay the long burden down,
For she is there awake when I'm alone,
Who cannot sleep, yet sorely, sorely would—
Oh, not in solitude!

Now everywhere I'm blind;
On the far journeys
Toward the magical old trees and cities
It's the same rooted sorrow that I find,
And everywhere I'm blind.

Is there a human prayer
That might unknot prolonged
Unnatural grief, grief that has surely wronged
Her very radiant presence in the air,
Is there a human prayer?

It is poor love, I know,
Mother and marvelous friend,
Over that final poverty to bend
And not remember all the rich life too:
It is poor love, I know.

"Rich love, come in,
Come home, my treasure.
All that you were and that no word can measure

Melt itself through me like a healing balm,
Rich love, come home."

And here lay down at last
Her long hard death,
And let her be in joy, be ash, not breath,
And let her gently go into the past,
Dear world, to rest at last.

After the laboring birth, the clean stripped hull
Glides down the ways and is gently set free,
The landlocked, launched; the cramped made bountiful—
Oh, grave great moment when ships take the sea!
Alone now in my life, no longer child,
This hour and its flood of mystery,
Where death and love are wholly reconciled,
Launches the ship of all my history.
Accomplished now is the last struggling birth,
I have slipped out from the embracing shore
Nor look for comfort to maternal earth.
I shall not be a daughter any more,
But through this final parting, all stripped down,
Launched on the tide of love, go out full grown.

I never saw my father old;
I never saw my father cold.
His stride, staccato, vital,
His talk struck from pure metal
Simple as gold, and all his learning
Only to light a passion's burning.
So, beaming like a lesser god,
He bounced upon the earth he trod,
And people marvelled on the street
At this stout man's impetuous feet.

Loved donkeys, children, awkward ducks,
Loved to retell old simple jokes;
Lived in a world of innocence
Where loneliness could be intense;
Wrote letters until very late,
Found comfort in an orange cat—
Rufus and George exchanged no word,
But while George worked his Rufus purred—
And neighbors looked up at his light
Warmed by the scholar working late.

I never saw my father passive;
He was electrically massive.
He never hurried, so he said,
And yet a fire burned in his head;
He worked as poets work, for love,
And gathered in a world alive,
While black and white above his door
Spoke Mystery, the avatar—
An Arabic inscription flowed
Like singing: "In the name of God."

And when he died, he died so swift
His death was like a final gift.
He went out when the tide was full,
Still undiminished, bountiful;

The scholar and the gentle soul,
The passion and the life were whole.
And now death's wake is only praise,
As when a neighbor writes and says:
"I did not know your father, but
His light was there. I miss the light."

Did someone say there would be an end,
An end, Oh an end to love and mourning?
Such voices speak when sleep and waking blend,
The cold bleak voices of the early morning
When all the birds are dumb in dark November,
Remember and forget, forget, remember.

After the false night, warm true voices, wake!
Voice of the dead that touches the cold living,
Through the pale sunlight once more gravely speak.
Tell me again while the last leaves are falling:
"Dear child, what has been once so interwoven
Cannot be ravelled, nor the gift ungiven."

Now the dead move through all of us still glowing,
Mother and child, lover and lover mated
Are wound and bound together and enflowing.
What has been plaited cannot be unplaited—
Only the strands grow richer with each loss,
And memory makes kings and queens of us.

Darkness to light, light into darkness spin.
When all the birds have flown to some real haven,
We who find shelter in the warmth within,
Listen, and feel new-cherished, new-forgiven,
As the lost human voices speak through us and blend
Our complex love, our mourning without end.

NATIVITY

(Piero della Francesca)

O cruel cloudless space,
And pale bare ground where the poor infant lies!
Why do we feel restored
As in a sacramental place?
Here Mystery is artifice,
And here a vision of such peace is stored,
Healing flows from it through our eyes.

Comfort and joy are near,
Not as we know them in the usual ways,
Personal and expected,
But utterly distilled and spare
Like a cool breath upon the air.
Emotion, it would seem, has been rejected
For a clear geometric praise.

Even the angels' stance
Is architectural in form:
They tell no story.
We read on each grave countenance,
Withheld as in a formal dance,
The awful joy, the serene glory:
And we have heard, and we are warm.

Poised as a monument,
Thought rests; and in these balanced spaces
Images meditate;
Whatever Piero meant,
The strange impersonal does not relent:
Here is Love, naked, lying in great state
On the bare ground, as in all human faces.

As it is brought in with its coat
Smelling of wilderness and yet not furry,
It still has an untamed look,
As if it might crash the ceiling
Or lie down in a corner and refuse
All welcome, an unwilling prisoner.
Small children and animals are wary
For fear it might break out or simply die,
Until it is time to set it up on end,
Sturdy, sweet-smelling, and so high
It makes a shelter and becomes a friend.

This is the moment to uncover
In boxes so light, what can they hold?—
From softest tissue to unwrap and gather
The apples of silver, the apples of gold.
Now gently deck the boughs, gently unfurl
The sprung branch that will wear
This lightest jewel in its pungent fur.
Is it real? Will it stay? Has it come
From so far, long ago, just to bloom
Just tonight, heart's desire, in this room?
The candles are lit, one by one, very slowly.
All gaze; all are silent; each child is holy.

The smallest in pajamas goes and lies
Under the boughs with wholly dazzled eyes,
And as he looks up at the gaudy toys
They become strange and spiritual joys,
While the tree, stranger once from wilderness,
Is an angelic presence that can bless;
And all wound round now with the blazing truth,
The boy, the tree together are redeeming myth.

To The Living

WHO WAKES

(Detroit, June, 1943)

Who wakes now who lay blind with sleep?
Who starts, bright-eyed with anger from his bed?
I do. I, the plain citizen. I cannot sleep.
I hold the torturing fire in my head.

I, an American, call the dead Negro's name,
And in the hot dark of the city night
I walk the streets alone and sweat with shame.
Too late to rise, to raise the dead too late.

This is the harvest. The seeds sown long ago—
The careless word, sly thought, excusing glance.
I reap now everything I let pass, let go.
This is the harvest of my own indifference.

I, the plain citizen, have grown disorder
In my own world. It is not what I meant.
But dreams and images are potent and can murder.
I stand accused of them. I am not innocent.

Can I now plant imagination, honesty,
And love where violence and terror were unbound,
The images of hope, the dream's responsibility?

Those who died here were murdered in my mind.

Cried Innocence, "Mother, my thumbs, my thumbs!
The pain will make me wild."
And Wisdom answered, "Your brother-man
Is suffering, my child."

Screamed Innocence, "Mother, my eyes, my eyes!
Someone is blinding me."
And Wisdom answered, "Those are your brother's eyes,
The blinded one is he."

Cried Innocence, "Mother, my heart, my heart!
It bursts with agony."
And Wisdom answered, "That is your brother's heart
Breaking upon a tree."

Screamed Innocence, "Mother, I want to die.
I cannot bear the pain."
And Wisdom answered, "They will not let him die.
They bring him back again."

Cried Innocence, "Mother, I cannot bear
It now. My flesh is wild!"
And Wisdom answered, "His agony is endless
For your sake, my child."

Then whispered Innocence, "Mother, forgive,
Forgive my sin, forgive—"
And Wisdom wept. "Now do you understand, Love,
How you must live?"

We ask the peace of the spirit for each other,
A more difficult one than mere not-strife,
The tired enemy beside his brother,
Possessing at last, but in sleep, his ardent life.

We ask something more arduous and deeper
Than calm suspension of the warring blood,
Than death-likeness of an unconscious sleeper.
We ask a living peace where warriors stood.

Peace as we dream it is a wingèd strain:
Do you remember Victory on the stairs?
She who has lost her arms, poised and alone,
Still looks as if an unconquerable world were hers—

Though she stands broken and no ship behind her.

(for Lugné-Poe, founder of the Oeuvre Theatre in Paris)

At sixty-five said, "I fight every day.
My dear, nothing but death will stop
My uninterrupted élan in the play."
Then wrote, "When I am forced to see
What happens to our old humanity,
All seems ignoble and I rage
To have been listed player on this stage."
At sixty-five that anger conquered fear:
The old man raged, but he did not despair.

At sixty-seven then he laughed and said,
"My dear, how proud I am of all the haters
Who stand behind and wish that I were dead,"
Those who had tasted of his honesty,
Those usurers of mediocrity—
At sixty-seven he refused to praise
(And lost his job) their rotten little plays.
But when he told me how he shouted there,
The old man laughed, but he did not despair.

He said at seventy, "But we must work, my dear.
I see a certain look upon their faces.
Discouragement? Perhaps I dream it there.
The wicked times have put me back to school,
And I shall die a sensitive young fool.
The news is doing me to death at last."
And then a note, "The evil eats me fast.
You must help men not to be slaves, my dear!"
(The old man died, but he did not despair.)

If the one certainty is suffering,
And if the only absolute is doubt,
From these alone belief must be wrung
Or else the bitter poverty found out:
Take anguish for companion and set out.

It leads us back to man himself to sit
Down by his side whom we have killed and starved,
Brother and sister, criminal and half-wit,
For each of us there is a place reserved
To sit beside the one we have not served.

Wake as he dreams, dream as he wakes to see
Man always at our side, starving and weeping,
Curved like a mother over his misery,
Huge and abandoned like a giant sleeping,
And we ourselves this creature we are keeping.

But if we dare to keep anguish companion,
We feel spring in our throats a living song,
See man leap from the rocks toward the sun,
Refuse to be imprisoned for too long,
His anger storming at the walls of wrong.

He is suddenly willing joy instead of power,
Shaken to the marrow by joy as by a flame,
Bending with mad delight toward a flower,
Secret and tender, violent, he came
Up from the darkness toward his haunting name.

He is the one who always sings and cries,
Believes in spite of every proof he will
Out of the darkness see with clearer eyes,
Conquer himself and learn to be an angel,
Who finds his only peace within the struggle.

For to be desperate is to discover strength.
We die of comfort and by conflict live,
Who grow in this knowledge till at length
We find it good, find it belief enough
To be anguish alive, creating love.

1

How faint the horn sounds in the mountain passes
Where folded in the folds of memory
All the heroic helmets lie in summer grasses,
Who wore them vanished utterly.

How dry the blood on ancient cross and stone
Where folded in the folds of memory
The martyrs cry out where each falls alone
In his last faithful agony.

How fresh and clear the stains of human weeping
Where folded in the folds of memory
The millions who have died for us are sleeping
In our long tragic history.

2

The need to kill what is unknown and strange
Whether it be a poem or an ancient race,
The fear of thought, fear of experience
That might demand some radical heart-change—
These are the mountains that hem a narrow place
Out of the generous plains of our inheritance:
Speak to the children of the world as whole,
Whole as the heart that can include it all,
And of the fear of thought as the first sin;
Tell them the revolution is within.

Open the mind, and the whole earth and sky
Are freed from fear to be explored and known.
Nothing so strange it does not hold delight
Once it is seen with clear and naked eye.
The thinking man will never be alone—
He travels where he sits, his heart alight:
Speak to the children of a living Greece
As real as Texas, and the whole earth a place

Where everywhere men hope and work to be
More greatly human, and responsible, and free.

Tell them the deepest changes rise like rivers
From hearts of men long dead; tell them that we
Are borne now on the currents of their faith,
The saints and martyrs and all great believers,
As well at Rome with Paul as at Thermopylae:
Our freedom rises from the body of this death.
Tell them the rivers are rich to overflowing,
And, as we love our fraction of the past in growing,
These floods of change are to be loved and cherished;
That we may live, millions of men have perished.

Give them their rich, their full inheritance:
Open the whole past, and see the future plain—
The long treks across China, all the voyages.
Look deep and know these were not done by chance.
Look far enough ahead and see the fruits of pain,
And see the harvests of all pilgrimages:
Speak to the children now of revolution,
Not as a violence, a terror, and a dissolution,
But as the long-held hope and the long dream of man,
The river in his heart and his most pure tradition.

INNUMERABLE FRIEND

"Ainsi du temple où seul l'ami entre,
mais innombrable"
—Saint-Exupéry

Let us forget these principalities,
Nations, governments, these mythical powers,
These real walls, these beleaguered cities;
We are theirs, perhaps, but they are not ours.
We move and must move always one by one
Across the perilous frontiers alone,
And what we build be builded severally.
But who are "we" and is there still a "we"
Not lost under the weight of history?
The poet, scientist, and teacher know
How fast the seeds of hate and fear can grow,
What passions can take over peaceful nations,
What anguish lurk in the safe reservations.
Can we not start at the small roots again,
Build this "we" slowly, gently, one by one,
From each small center toward communion?
Reach over the frontier stranger to stranger
To find the only sure relief from danger.
Take the immense dangerous leap to understand,
Build an invisible bridge from mind to mind;
Swung out from letters or the briefest meeting
(Lives have been changed by a simple greeting),
Build an invisible bridge toward one person.
So the slow delicate process is begun,
The root of all relationship, and then
Learn that this stranger has become all men,
Flows through the open heart as a great host
Of all the human, solitary, lost.
His longing streams through the conventions
Of diplomats and their meagre intentions,
Hunting for home like a great hungry wind.
He is the one, this our innumerable friend!

Let us forget these principalities, these powers;
We are theirs perhaps, but they are not ours.
Turn toward each other quietly and know
There are still bridges nations cannot overthrow.
And if we fight—if we must at the end—
These are the bridges we fight to defend.

A painting by Chirico: "The Delights of the Poet"

Here space, time, peace are given a habitation,
Perspective of pillar and arch, shadow on light,
A luminous evening where it can never be night.
This is the pure splendor of imagination.

To hold eternally present and forever still
The always fugitive, to make the essence clear,
Compose time and the moment as shadow in a square,
As these pure arches have been composed by will.

As by a kind of absence, feat of super-session,
We can evoke a face long-lost, long lost in death,
Or those hidden now in the wilderness of oppression—
Know the immortal breath upon the mortal breath:

A leaping out of the body to think, the sense
Of absence that precedes the stern work of creation.
Now when the future depends on our imagination,
Remember these pure arches and their imminence.

New Poems

1

Now these two warring halves are to be parted,
And the long struggle to anneal, come through
To where divided love could grow whole-hearted
Is given over. Now we are cut in two.
Never will you and I meet face to face,
Never again, you say, upon this ground,
So our last battle was a special grace—
An ether to anaesthetize the wound.
When we are conscious, we shall understand
Better perhaps just how it can be done,
How surgeons crack apart the tight-clasped hand,
What scalpel can unknot love at the bone.
The surgeon's name is Reason. We shall see
How Reason operates on Poetry.

2

I shall not see the end of this unweaving.
I shall lie dead in any narrow ditch
Before they are unwoven, love and grieving,
And our lives separated stitch by stitch.
I shall be dead before this task is done,
Not for a moment give you your cool head:
Say we had twenty years and now have none,
Are you Old Fate itself to snap the thread,
And to cut both your life and mine in half
Before the whole design is written clear?
This tapestry will not unweave itself,
Nor I spend what is left of me to tear
Your bright thread out: let unfulfilled design
Stand as your tragic epitaph, and mine.

3

One death's true death, and that is,—not to care.
We do not die of feeling, even the extreme
Great arc of tension we had learned to bear;
I woke once out of a disturbing dream:
I could not reach you. You were lost and cold.
And the worst was I did not even mind,
Distant myself, and tired like the old—
But then you woke and tender love was kind.
Now you condemn us to wake up alone
Without a human breast on which to lie
Until we sleep at last against a stone,
Still let me say I live and shall not die:
When you kill love and reason mystery,
You have condemned yourself to death, not me.

4

Did you achieve this with a simple word?
Chase out the furies and the plagues of passion,
Cut through the shapes of conscience with your sword
And make your peace in such a ruthless fashion?
I wonder what the weapon really was,
It is so windless here, so very still,
And we move through our palaces of glass
As freezing cold as if this world were Hell.
My guess is that the weapon's name was Pride.
It is a word the Furies understand;
Their ghosts are gathering on every side,
And they will raise the hair upon your hand.
For who can punish ghosts or give them warning?
They will be there at night, and in the morning.

5

What price serenity these cruel days?
Your silence and ungiving, my small cries,
Followed by hours when I can lift some praise
And make the wound sing as in Paradise.
What price the poise you ask for, the unharried?
Four rooted years torn up without a qualm,
A past not dead perhaps, but quickly buried:
On one side anguish, on the other calm,
Both terrible because deprived of hope
Like living eyes still open in a grave.
And we shall lunch, you say, that is our scope.
Between what we have lost and still might save
Lies, very quiet, what was once too human,
And lovely, and beloved, a living woman.

6

Dear fellow-sufferer, dear cruelty,
"I feel so married to you," once you said,
And it is you who now unmarry me.
I wish I could hold fast your tired head,
Or bind up all the wounds that we have made,
Say that I never hurt, you never saddened,
Say we were good and peaceful, undismayed—
The truth is that we always wounded, maddened,
Tore every joy out of such pain, it is
No wonder that the battle nearly killed.
From such inhuman ways you wish to save us:
Oh, is it better now, all anguish stilled?
Tell me what sovereign remedy you found
To call this better, this one mortal wound?

7

Your greatness withers when it shuts out grief
And must assert itself through the denying
Of what was lately sap and the green leaf,
And this new stance resembles only dying.
Castrati have pure voices, as we know,
But the mature who mutilate by choice,
Who cut the heart out so that they may grow,
What sweetness flows from such a tortured voice?
So you would gather in and cherish power,
"Today I have grown old," is your decree;
You cut down passion like a summer flower,
And chill the ripening season's warmth in me,
Whose strength was wiser when you could enfold
Another in your arms against the cold.

8

Now we have lost the heartways and the word,
Our senses blinded, our five wits too numb,
Like planes that circle, or a blundering bird
That cannot chart the clouded skies for home.
Now rocked and hurtled through the empty spaces,
We hang upon the hope that some thin radar
May light from deep within our darkened faces,
And tell us what to do, and where we are;
Focus the awful blurring of the dream,
And give some destination to the heart.
What can it tell us, that deep inward beam,
How write a new course on this troubled chart?
Will this lost journey never have an end
Nor the skies open so that love may land?

What if a homing pigeon lost its home,
Were wrenched out of the orbit of sensation,
Its instinct killed, what would it then become?
A haunted traveller with no destination,
Circling the air above strange roosts to climb
Upward again, more fearful, more harassed,
The gentle voice repeating all the time
The phrases that had meaning in the past,
"Where is my true love, O where is my nest?
Where can I shut this terrible bright eye
And put my head under a wing to rest?"
That baffled wanderer, that lost one, I
Who for a whole month now have flown and flown,
And cannot land find my own.

It does not mean that we shall find the place
Called peaceable in the old hopeful prints
Where every tiger has a human face,
And every lamb can make a lion wince—
We met too late to know our meeting kind,
Too late for me to educate your heart,
Too late for you to educate my mind.
We shall be hurt again, and badly hurt;
There are torrents we cannot ever wall,
And there are arid deserts still to cross.
We shall not come where the green mercies fall,
To perfect grace, nor forget cruel loss—
But if we turn back now in such distress,
How find the way out ... ...lderness?

13

Wild seas, wild seas, and the gulls veering close;
Dark islands float upon the silver Sound;
This weather is too sombre for repose,
And I suffer the truth I have not found
As gulls suffer the wind and ride it too:
The speechless battle with the inner weather
That longs only to end with peace in you:
Oh, when you struck me did you strike your mother?
Did I strike back to come into the dream?
(Nothing but storm and the wild seas today)
No wonder you withdrew and I still scream:
What present riches did we throw away
To act the ancient drama out until
The past and we cracked open and stood still?

14

For all the loving words and difficult
Work on the unregenerate heart, we foundered
Upon the seaming of a secret fault,
As rocks, mined by a flaw, are slowly sundered.
The need that joined us was too young and strong,
Yielding to violence and rage too soon,
Our every insight wrenched from some weak wrong.
This adult passion cried for a child's moon.
Not all the tenderness could set us free,
Nor all the steadfast hope through all the pain:
You never have been, you will never be
(The rock falls here, the secret flaw is plain)
My father, nor my son, nor any kin.
Where these words end, let solitude begin.

15

As I look out on the long swell of fields
Where winter wheat grows sparsely through the snow
And all lies fallow for those later yields,
Abandoned, quiet, where the pheasants go;
As skies move in slow motion overhead
To launch the wind and rain in a long gust,
Cold waves of air breaking on every homestead,
I beg my heart to lie still at long last.
But it thuds on, this animal gone blind,
And still enduring what strange marathon?
I must regard it with an acid mind:
Have done, poor beast, I say to it, have done,
And let pure thought rest on the winter sky
Without your stubborn question and reply.

16

The cat sleeps on my desk in the pale sun;
Long bands of light lie warm across the floor.
I have come back into my world of no one,
This house where the long silences restore
The essence and to time its real dimension;
All I have lost or squandered I examine
Free of the wars and the long searing tension;
And I am nourished here after the famine.
Though this was time that we had planned to spend
Together, circled on the calendars,
To walk my woods for one single week-end,
Last night I looked alone at the bright stars.
Nor time, nor absence breaks this world in two.
You hold me in your heart, as I hold you.

17

After a night of driving rain, the skies
Take on bright motion, radiant-obscure;
As thoughts like clouds traverse my human eyes,
Silence opens the world that I explore:
Mozartian gaiety, the lightest presence,
At last I welcome back my wandering soul
Into these regions of the strange transcendence,
And find myself again, alive and whole;
Now intimations of a joy so pure
It needs no human love to rest upon
Come to me from the airs and re-assure:
As I make the great leap to the unknown,
The flower of courage is given back to me,
Exact equivalent of agony.

18

These riches burst from every barren tree;
The brilliant mosses under balsam tell
All I have lost is given back to me,
And, naked as a newborn babe, I feel
The slightest change of air as an event,
Attend to every creak of the old floor
As to momentous words by angels sent,
Inner and outer worlds, mine to explore.
Take loneliness, take pain, and take it all!
Like some strong swimmer on the icy airs,
I glide and can survive the heart's own pitfall.
I tell you, I grow rich on these despairs:
For you I gladly yielded up my world,
Who now among enormous skies am hurled.

19

Where do I go? Nowhere. And who am I
Who sit alone in this small silent ark?
No one and no thing, but a breath or sigh,
Receptacle of light and flooding dark.
Now sunlight ripples through me in long waves,
Now the night rises, a tremendous tide,
And I am drowned or nearly. Then what saves?
Who is the bridegroom of this ghostly bride?
A thinking heart, a feeling mind stripped bare
Of warmth and flesh, the soft delight and thong,
Reduced to a fine bone, as thin and spare,
I may now make an instrument for song:
Poetry, pour through me your ruthless word
As strong as once was love that used me hard.

20

Now silence, silence, silence, and within it
The leap of spirit upward and beyond;
We take the heart's world in our hands and spin it
Out to the distant stars above this ground,
And let it go at last, and let it go
With those illusions that we held too long;
Against our will now we are forced to grow
And push out from all safety into song.
This is one half of it, the saving grace;
The other, the dark struggle, as, like worms
We riddle darkness, tunnel some small space
Where we can lie with patience through the storms.
And of these two, who knows where wisdom lies,
Deep in the earth, or wandering the skies?

I moved into my house one day
In a downpour of leaves and rain,
"I took possession," as they say,
With solitude for my domain.

At first it was an empty place
Where every room I came to meet
Watched me in silence like a face:
I heard the whisper of my feet.

So huge the absence walking there
Beside me on the yellow floor,
That one fly buzzing on the air
But made the stillness more and more.

What I possessed was all my own,
Yet not to be possessed at all,
And not a house or even hearthstone,
And never any sheltering wall.

There solitude became my task,
No shelter but a grave demand,
And I must answer, never ask,
Taking this bridegroom by the hand.

I moved into my life one day
In a downpour of leaves in flood,
I took possession as they say,
And knew I was alone for good.

REFLECTIONS BY A FIRE

(On moving into an old house in New Hampshire)

Fire is a good companion for the mind;
Here in this room, mellowed by sunlight, kind
After yesterday's thrall of rain and dark,
I watch the fire and feel some warm thoughts spark,
The seethe and bubble of some curious questions;
The air is full of small smiling suggestions.
For instance, why should window mouldings lead
To ruminations upon love and need?
As if in their proportions, cleanly limned
By some plain craftsman, values had been framed
That tease us and have never been explained.

These windows frame a world, the rural scene
We lift our heads to scan, the village green,
Church spire, dirt road curving toward the hill:
Windows select the form and hold it still.
Almost their shape defines the shape of thought,
That spaciousness in a small region caught.
I wonder if the secret of dimension
Will come to me if I can pay attention,
And if I chose this house because I guessed—
And hoped that I would pass the crucial test—
That if the form was there I'd learn the rest.

Here now, rooted at last in my own home,
The small, intimate, dreamed-of kingdom come,
I ponder an old theme beside the fire—
How untraditional is the desire
That moulds the great traditions of the mind,
For it is revolution that I find
(What strong belief structured the pillared doorway!)
Become the guest of old ideas at play,
Reason and passion, freedom and tradition.
A changing style adapts a revolution,
And window mouldings speak to man's condition.

Here private worlds rose to a grandeur given;
Men of this house left their dear hardwon haven
And travelled many a lonely dusty mile
Because they represented an old style,
Because they stood by a form in the mind,
(These doors and windows shape a man, and bind)
Knew what they meant and kept the meaning warm,
Taciturn, took a century by storm,
"Average, divine, original, concrete,"
Embodied freedom from a village street:
It is their ghosts I recognize and greet.

My windows frame a different world and season,
But here alive is passion and is reason.
The plain strong style supports my need to win
Some of its freedom and its discipline,
If not enlightenment, at least a tone
(Kind hopes that simmer in a house alone).
I dare myself within this native shell
To live close to the marrow, weather well,
Structure the bursts of love and poetry
So that both life and art may come to be
As strict and spacious as this house to me.

In early spring, so much like a late autumn,
Gray stubble and the empty trees,
We must contend with an unwieldy earth.
In this rebirth that feels so much like dying,
When the bare patches bleed into raw mud,
In rain, in coarsening ooze, we have grown sluggard,
Cold to the marrow with spring's non-arrival:
To hold what we must hold is iron-hard,
And strength is needed for the mere survival.

By dogged labor we must learn to lift
Ourselves and bring a season in;
No one has ever called child-bearing easy,
And this spring-bearing also asks endurance.
We are strained hard within our own becoming,
Forced to learn ways how to renew, restore.
Though we were dazzled once by perfect snow,
What we have not has made us what we are.
Those surface consolations have to go.

In early spring, so much a fall of will,
We struggle through muds of unreason,
We dig deep into caring and contention;
The cold unwieldy earth resists the spade.
But we contend to bring a difficult birth
Out from the lack of talent, partial scope,
And every failure of imagination.
Science and art and love still be our hope!
What we are not drives us to consummation.

Conflict has been our climate for so long,
All we know gleaned from high jagged places,
And not a question there of right or wrong,
But only foothold on the mountain faces,
A balance for the self upon those sheer
Dizzying cliffs, then crampon, creep on somehow
To where we came to master at least fear;
In this way learned the little that we know:
And managed to exist, following hunches,
Acutely wary of the avalanches.

How then accept this ultimate plateau,
The calm arrival after the harsh climb?
For here we must learn simply how to grow,
Now we are safely balanced. There is time.
The self is gardener and not mountaineer,
Handles a spade or hoe, scatters new seed,
No wish for stronghold now there is no fear,
But to learn joy as well as rooted need.

A strange, a different virtue is required
Here where the winds are kind, the temperate sun
Brings slowly up the green shoots we desired,
Now there is grace, and desperation gone.
Dear love, here we are planting—and so high,
Close to the cloud, visited by the snow—
A human world consoled by a great sky,
How grow from peace all that we wish to grow?
It is no small task. At last we have come
To plant our anguish and make for it a home.

The white walls of this airy house assume
Flowers as natural and needed friends;
All summer long while flowers are in bloom
Attentive expectation never ends—
The day begins with walking through wet grass
In a slow progress, to visit the whole garden,
And all is undecided as I pass,
For here I must be thief and also warden:
What must I leave? What can I bear to plunder?
What fragile freshness, what amazing throat
Has opened in the night, what single wonder
That will be sounded like a single note
When these light wandering thoughts deploy
Before the grave deeds of decisive joy?

Later, I cut judiciously and fill my basket.
It's a fine clamor of unrelated voices,
As I begin the day's adventure and slow task,
The delicate, absorbing task of choices—
That lavender and pink that need some acid,
Perhaps a saffron zinnia, linen-crisp?
Or poppy's crinkle beside the rich and placid
Rose petal, and some erratic plume or wisp
To enhance cosmos, its flat symmetry,
And always the poised starry phlox in masses—
Sometimes I have undone the same bouquet
A dozen times in six different glasses,
A dozen times and still dissatisfied,
As if that day my wish had been denied.

Sometimes two poppies can compose a world,
Two and one seed-pagoda on a hairy stem,
Blood-red, vermilion, each entity unfurled,
Clashes its cymbals in the silent room;
The scale so small, substance diaphanous,
Yet the reverberation of that twofold red
Has focussed one room for me ever since,
As if an Absolute had once been said.

Sometimes the entire morning does get lost
In ochres, greenish-whites, in warm deep rose,
As I pick all the zinnias against frost:
Salmon, crude red, magenta, and who knows
What harsh loud chords of music sweep the room?
Both chords and discords, till the whole bright thing
Explodes into a brilliant cloud of bloom,
And the white walls themselves begin to sing.

And so the morning's gone. Was this to waste it
In a long foolish flowery meditation?
Time slides away, and how are we to taste it?
Within the floating world all is sensation.
And yet I see eternity's long wink
In these elusive games, and only there:
When I can so suspend myself to think,
I seem suspended in undying air.

It is the light, of course, and its great ways;
It comes like a celestial charity
With warmth not coldness in its clarity,
And through the violent green its violet rays
Anatomize each single leaf to shine,
The flesh transparent to the nerves' design.

A blade of grass, a frond of goldenrod,
A branch of beech paled to translucent green,
This is a world where structure counts again,
Flooded through by the presence of the god.
These simple days are coursed by a great cry,
A storm of radiance sweeping from the sky.

And when it takes a crimson petal up,
The lifeblood shows so brilliant in the vein,
A single flower dominates the green,
As if all earth were lifted in this cup,
And life began to flow the other way,
Up from the brimming petal to the sky . . .

As if the echoing rocks were to reflect,
And every open meadow to fulfill
The place and time where dancing growth is still,
And light and structure gently intersect;
Not the cold but the warmth of *caritas*
Shows us the summer green for what it was.

The autumn light X-rays our sealed-up riches;
We find within the mullein its soft milk,
The folded seeds in parachutes of silk
That will fly soon to fall on fields and ditches.
Passionate summer's hour of proof is come:
Go we, my love, and catch a falling sun!

Now frost has broken summer like a glass,
This house and I resume our conversations;
The floors whisper a message as I pass,
I wander up and down these empty rooms
That have become my intimate relations,
Brimmed with your presence where your absence blooms—
And did you come at last, come home to tell
How all fulfillment tastes of a farewell?

Here is the room where you lay down full length
That whole first day, to read, and hardly stirred
As if arrival had taken all your strength;
Here is the table where you bent to write
The morning through, and silence spoke its word;
And here beside the fire we talked, as night
Came slowly from the wood across the meadow
To frame half of our brilliant world in shadow.

The rich fulfillment came; we held it all;
Four years of struggle brought us to this season,
Then in one week our summer turned to fall;
The air chilled and we sensed the chill in us,
The passionate journey ending in sweet reason.
The autumn light was there, frost on the grass.
And did you come at last, come home to tell
How all fulfillment tastes of a farewell?

Departure is the constant at this stage;
And all we know is that we cannot stop,
However much the childish heart may rage.
We are still outward-bound to obligations
And, radiant centers, life must drink us up,
Devour our strength in multiple relations.
Yet I still question in these empty rooms
Brimmed with your presence where your absence blooms,

What stays that can outlast these deprivations?
Now peopled by the dead, and ourselves dying,
The house and I resume old conversations:
What stays? Perhaps some autumn tenderness,
A different strength that forbids youthful sighing.
Though frost has broken summer like a glass,
Know, as we hear the thudding apples fall,
Not ripeness but the suffering change is all.